ABUNDANT TRUTH INTERNATIONAL MINISTRIES

Prophetic Studies Series

PROPHETIC CLARITY

Exploring Questions & Answers for the Prophetic Office and Gift

Published by Abundant Truth Publishing
P.O. Box 126
Camden, NC 27921
Web: www.abundantpublishing.net
Email: abundantpublishing@gmail.com

Printed U.S.A.

Front & Back Cover Designs by Abundant Truth Publishing
All rights reserved.
Image by Tung Lam from Pixabay

Abundant Truth Publishing is a ministry of **Abundant Truth International Ministries.** The primary mission of ATI Ministries is to equip the Body of Christ with tools necessary to defend and contend for the truth of the Christian faith. Jesus Christ came to bear witness of the truth and ATI Ministries is a modern-day extension of His commission (John 18:37).

Abundant Truth Spiritual Gifts Series –Prophetic Clarity
©2024 Abundant Truth Publishing
All Rights Reserved
ISBN13: 978-1-60141-623-0

Unless otherwise indicated, all of the scripture quotations are taken from the *Authorized King James Version* **of the Bible.** Scripture quotations marked with NIV are taken from the *New International Version* **of the Bible. Scripture quotations marked with NASV are taken from the** *New American Standard Version* **of the Bible. Scripture quotations marked with Amplified are taken from the** *Amplified Bi*

Printed in the United States of America

Contents

Introduction

Question 1   1

Can someone prophesy at will?

Question 2   5

Is prophecy the same as preaching?

Question 3   9

If a prophecy is not clear, does it make it invalid?

Question 4   13

Are all prophecies conditional?

Question 5   17

Can someone impart the gift of prophecy to another?

Question 6   21

Can someone prophesy without the gift of prophecy?

Question 7   25

Is prophecy a gift that one is born with?

Contents *(cont.)*

Question 8   29
Does scripture negate the operation of personal prophecy?

Question 9   33
Does having the gift of prophecy make me a prophet?

Question 10   37
Can women be called to the prophetic office?

Question 11   41
Is the gift of prophecy only concerned with the future?

Question 12   45
Can someone be called as a prophet and do not have the gift of prophecy?

Question 13   49
If I desire the gift of prophecy, will God give it to me?

Contents *(cont.)*

Question 14   53

If my parents are prophets and/or have the gift of prophecy, does that make me a prophet? Will I have the gift of prophecy?

Question 15   57

How Can I Judge Personal Prophetic Words?

Bibliography   69

Introduction

The promise of the Father was the outpouring of the Holy Spirit. In Joel's prophecy, he said the prophetic revelation, dreams, and visions would be the outward demonstration of Spirit's coming. Therefore, prophetic revelation and ministry is a permanent feature of the New Testament Church. The Prophetic Studies Series was designed to inform and encourage the believer in prophetic manifestations and demonstrations in the Church. It is our prayer that believers will acknowledge, accept, and appreciate the prophetic ministry today.

In this publication:

The gift of prophecy and the prophetic office are God's gift to the New Testament Church. However, controversy and confusion still permeate the Body of Christ.

In this publication, we will address prevalent questions and provide pertinent answers surrounding prophetic manifestations. It is our prayer that a greater understand and appreciation for prophetic operations will be accomplished.

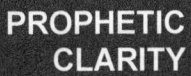

PROPHETIC CLARITY Exploring Questions & Answers for the Prophetic Office and Gift

-Question 1-

Can someone prophesy at will?

PROPHETIC CLARITY
Exploring Questions & Answers for the Prophetic Office and Gift

Prophetic Studies Series 2

PROPHETIC CLARITY — Exploring Questions & Answers for the Prophetic Office and Gift

The answer to this question is No. When we prophesy, we speak for another. Prophecy comes from God, alone.

*For the prophecy came not in old time by the will of man: but holy men of God spake as **they were moved** by the Holy Ghost. (2 Peter 2:21 Emphasis Mine)*

Though we can stir up the gifts of God on the inside, it is based upon the will of God when prophecy is received and ministered.

 Exploring Questions & Answers for the Prophetic Office and Gift

PROPHETIC CLARITY Exploring Questions & Answers for the Prophetic Office and Gift

-Question 2-

Is prophecy the same as preaching?

PROPHETIC CLARITY

Exploring Questions & Answers for the Prophetic Office and Gift

Though there are similar functions between these two ministries, prophecy is not the same as preaching. Preaching is designed to convert men to the knowledge of the truth.

> *For after that in the wisdom of God the world by wisdom knew not God, it pleased God by the foolishness of preaching to save them that believe. (I Corinthians 1:21)*

Prophecy helps men to continue in the truth presented through preaching. Preaching offers a general word for the masses. Conversely, prophecy comes to specific people for specific situations.

PROPHETIC CLARITY — Exploring Questions & Answers for the Prophetic Office and Gift

PROPHETIC CLARITY Exploring Questions & Answers for the Prophetic Office and Gift

-Question 3-

If a prophecy is not clear, does it make it invalid?

PROPHETIC CLARITY

Exploring Questions & Answers for the Prophetic Office and Gift

It is true that unclear prophecy may not be from the Lord.

*And even things without life giving **sound**, whether pipe or harp, except they give a distinction in the **sounds**, how shall it be known what is piped or harped? 8 For if the trumpet give an **uncertain sound**, who shall prepare himself to the battle? (I Corinthians 14:7-8)*

However, prophecy does come in part. God may send a seemingly vague prophecy in order to draw the hearer into prayer.

For we know in part, and we prophesy in part. (I Corinthians 13:9)

PROPHETIC CLARITY — Exploring Questions & Answers for the Prophetic Office and Gift

PROPHETIC CLARITY Exploring Questions & Answers for the Prophetic Office and Gift

-Question 4-
Are all prophecies conditional?

PROPHETIC CLARITY

Exploring Questions & Answers for the Prophetic Office and Gift

Prophetic Studies Series 14

Most personal prophecies are conditional. If we remain in Him and serve Him in faith, we will receive what the Lord promised.

If thou shalt hearken unto the voice of the Lord thy God, (Deuteronomy 30:10 Emphasis Mine)

Prophecies concerning God's eternal purpose are not conditional. They will happen according to His word.

Exploring Questions & Answers for the Prophetic Office and Gift

Exploring Questions & Answers for the Prophetic Office and Gift

-Question 5-

Can someone impart the gift of prophecy to another?

Exploring Questions & Answers for the Prophetic Office and Gift

Impartation can only take place by the will of God. He is the one who anoints and gives gifts. If He desires for someone to share in the anointing or gift in our life, He will allow an impartation. This is similar to Him taking Moses' spirit and placing it upon the elders. However, Moses did not do it; it was done by the will of God.

> *And the LORD said unto Moses, Gather unto me seventy men of the elders of Israel, whom thou knowest to be the elders of the people, and officers over them; and bring them unto the tabernacle of the congregation, that they may stand there with thee. And I will come down and talk with thee there: and I will take of the spirit which is upon thee, and will put it upon them; and they shall bear*

the burden of the people with thee, that thou bear it not thyself alone. (Deuteronomy 11:16-17)

If God does not plan for you to have a certain gift or ministry, no men can impart what they have. It has to be in God's will. Elisha could receive a double portion of Elijah's spirit because he was to replace him in the prophetic office. His reception of the mantle and double portion were in line with the calling of God upon his life.

In these instances, God gives us mentors and spiritual fathers/mothers to impart a portion of themselves into our lives, which will enhance the ministry already in us.

PROPHETIC CLARITY — Exploring Questions & Answers for the Prophetic Office and Gift

-Question 6-

Can someone prophesy without the gift of prophecy?

PROPHETIC CLARITY Exploring Questions & Answers for the Prophetic Office and Gift

Exploring Questions & Answers for the Prophetic Office and Gift

Yes. The Holy Spirit dwells in every believer but manifests Himself differently in each. Since He abides in the believer, He may see fit to use someone in a gift that he does not normally function in for a particular purpose.

And it shall come to pass afterward That I will pour out My Spirit on all flesh; Your sons and your daughters shall prophesy, Your old men shall dream dreams, Your young men shall see visions. Joel 2:28)

In addition, when the spirit of prophecy comes in the Church, any believer present will be able to prophesy.

PROPHETIC CLARITY

Exploring Questions & Answers for the Prophetic Office and Gift

Prophetic Studies Series 24

PROPHETIC CLARITY — Exploring Questions & Answers for the Prophetic Office and Gift

-Question 7-

Is prophecy a gift that one is born with?

No. Every spiritual gift is an endowment of the Spirit of the Lord. The Spirit gives gifts at His own will. Don't use Jeremiah's commission as a basis for this erroneous thought.

...and I ordained thee a prophet unto the nations. (Jeremiah 1:5)

He was **ordained** a prophet. He did not receive an endowment until the Lord laid His hands on his mouth (Jeremiah 1:9).

PROPHETIC CLARITY
Exploring Questions & Answers for the Prophetic Office and Gift

Exploring Questions & Answers for the Prophetic Office and Gift

-Question 8-

Does scripture negate the operation of personal prophecy?

No. Even after the Holy Ghost came and the Church was established, God gave individuals the gift of prophecy.

For to one is given by the Spirit the word of wisdom; to another the word of knowledge by the same Spirit; (I Corinthians 12:8)

If it was operational then, it still provides a great blessing to the Church today.

PROPHETIC CLARITY Exploring Questions & Answers for the Prophetic Office and Gift

PROPHETIC CLARITY — Exploring Questions & Answers for the Prophetic Office and Gift

-Question 9-

Does having the gift of prophecy make me a prophet?

PROPHETIC CLARITY Exploring Questions & Answers for the Prophetic Office and Gift

No. The gift of prophecy can be in any believer. It may be a sign of a prophetic calling. The prophet's call is more than the gift of prophecy, it is foundational to the Church.

And there are diversities of operations, but it is the same God which worketh all in all.
1 Corinthians 12:6

God calls them personally to service. If you have not experienced this, you may be called to operate solely in the gift of prophecy or a prophetic anointing.

PROPHETIC CLARITY
Exploring Questions & Answers for the Prophetic Office and Gift

Exploring Questions & Answers for the Prophetic Office and Gift

-Question 10-

Can women be called to the prophetic office?

Exploring Questions & Answers for the Prophetic Office and Gift

In the Old Testament, we have record of women being called to the prophetic office. Women such as Miriam, Huldah, and Deborah were called **prophetesses**.

> *So Hilkiah and those whom the king had sent[a] went to Huldah the **prophetess**, the wife of Shallum the son of Tokhath, son of Hasrah, keeper of the wardrobe (now she lived in Jerusalem in the Second Quarter) and spoke to her to that effect. (2 Chronicles 34:22)*

Since the prophetic ministry continues in the New Testament Church, then we know that women are still being called to this office.

PROPHETIC CLARITY Exploring Questions & Answers for the Prophetic Office and Gift

-Question 11-

Is the gift of prophecy only concerned with the future?

PROPHETIC CLARITY Exploring Questions & Answers for the Prophetic Office and Gift

No. The gift of prophecy is a 'now' word from the Lord. It brings us into the mind of God. It may contain predictive elements, though this is only a part of the manifestation of the gift of prophecy.

> *But he that prophesieth speaketh unto men to edification, and exhortation, and comfort. 1 Corinthians 14:3*

We know from biblical accounts prophecies also came to strengthen individuals in their walk with the Lord or give instructions from the mouth of God.

PROPHETIC CLARITY Exploring Questions & Answers for the Prophetic Office and Gift

PROPHETIC CLARITY Exploring Questions & Answers for the Prophetic Office and Gift

-Question 12-

Can someone be called as a prophet and do not have the gift of prophecy?

Exploring Questions & Answers for the Prophetic Office and Gift

No. This is why a prophet is called a prophet. His ministry is given to speak for or prophesy in the name of the Lord.

The prophet that hath a dream, let him tell a dream; and he that hath my word, let him speak my word faithfully. (Jeremiah 23:28)

He would not be able to perform His purpose without the gift of prophecy. Prophecy is the basis for the prophet's ministry.

PROPHETIC CLARITY
Exploring Questions & Answers for the Prophetic Office and Gift

PROPHETIC CLARITY — Exploring Questions & Answers for the Prophetic Office and Gift

-Question 13-

If I desire the gift of prophecy, will God give it to me?

Exploring Questions & Answers for the Prophetic Office and Gift

The scriptures tell us to ask God for the best gifts. He would not have told us to ask, if He did not intend to give us our request. If God denies your request for this gift, trust His wisdom. However, we can ask and expect to receive.

Wherefore, brethren, covet to prophesy, and forbid not to speak with tongues. (I Corinthians 14:39)

Paul instructed the believers to covet this manifestation of the Spirit.

PROPHETIC CLARITY — Exploring Questions & Answers for the Prophetic Office and Gift

-Question 14-

If my parents are prophets and/or have the gift of prophecy, does that make me a prophet? Will I have the gift of prophecy?

PROPHETIC CLARITY
Exploring Questions & Answers for the Prophetic Office and Gift

Not necessarily. The gifts and callings of God are based upon the discretion of the Lord, not family.

> *Before I formed thee in the belly I knew thee; and before thou camest forth out of the womb I sanctified thee, and I ordained thee a prophet unto the nations. Jeremiah 1:5*

Though God sometimes uses whole families in similar ministries, it is not the standard. Only God can reveal what gifts and callings you have, not family ties.

PROPHETIC CLARITY Exploring Questions & Answers for the Prophetic Office and Gift

-Question 15-

How Can I Judge Personal Prophetic Words?

(Adapted from "The Prophetic Mantle: The Gift of Prophecy and Prophetic Operations in the Church Today")

Exploring Questions & Answers for the Prophetic Office and Gift

PROPHETIC CLARITY — Exploring Questions & Answers for the Prophetic Office and Gift

There is much to consider in the delivery and reception of prophetic ministry. Thus, a proper perspective of prophetic ministry has to be developed. Without a proper prophetic perspective, individuals will begin to despise prophecy because of the errors of others.

> *Quench not the Spirit. Despise not prophesyings. Prove all things; hold fast that which is good. (I Thessalonians 5:19-21)*

When we distrust prophetic ministry, it results in a quenching of the Spirit. God delights in revealing His mind to us through the prophetic Spirit.

> *But as it is written, Eye hath not seen, nor ear heard, neither have entered into the heart of man, the things which God*

hath prepared for them that love him. But God hath revealed them unto us by his Spirit: for the Spirit searcheth all things, yea, the deep things of God. (I Corinthians 2:9-10)

In addition to despising prophecy, there are others who are afraid to trust prophecy. They fear that they will be misled. To walk in distrust and fear with regard to the prophetic ministry is not the will of God for the believer.

In this chapter, we will discuss how to avoid a major pitfalls in prophetic ministry; namely, in judging prophetic ministry.

Guidelines for Judging Prophecy

One of the major facets of understanding prophecy is to discern when something is not prophecy. Judging prophecy can be a tough task at times. Nevertheless, the scriptures do give guidelines to us to help us as we strive to hear from God through others. We all want to receive from God, but some of us have lost faith in the gift of prophecy.

Many have received erroneous prophecies. Others have followed the directions given to them through prophecy and the results were unfavorable. When judging a prophetic word, we must be careful not to miss God.

Conversely, we need to know when God has not spoken. If you are unsure as to how to hear from God through others, there are certain questions you can ask yourself. We must understand that God does speak to His people through this gift. We do not need to be afraid, but discerning.

 Exploring Questions & Answers for the Prophetic Office and Gift

Even if we have received bad prophetic words in the past, we should not allow the

enemy to steal a blessing from us. God may send someone with a valid prophetic word.

Does it come to pass? Sometimes this aspect of judging is hard to determine. However, if the person prophesying (prophet or laymen) gives a specific period or date for the word of the Lord to happen, it is easier to determine.

> *When a prophet speaketh in the name of the Lord, if the thing follow not, nor come to pass, that is the thing which the Lord hath not spoken, but the prophet hath spoken it presumptuously: thou shalt not be afraid of him. (Deuteronomy 18:22)*

Conversely, do not be quick to brand the prophecy false because it did not occur when you expected it. Prayerfully consider the word. It may turn out to be valid, but you did not understand the time in which it was to happen.

Is it clear and understandable? Though God speaks to us in strange ways at times, the word of the Lord should be understandable; else, you will not know what to do. You cannot obey God if the word is unclear.

> *For God is not the author of confusion, but of peace, as in all the churches of the saints. (I Corinthians 14:33)*

On the other hand, if you do not understand the word, ask the person who delivered the word for clarity. You may find that their choice of words was not clear rather than the prophecy being bogus. There may be times when the person prophesying may not know or remember what was said. However, it is our belief that if the word is from God, they should be able to explain more clearly what they received.

Does it agree with the Word? Prophecy will never instruct you to do something against the written word of God. The scriptures represent the purest expression of prophecy.

> *We have also a more sure word of prophecy; whereunto ye do well that ye take heed, as unto a light that shineth in a dark place, until the day of dawn, and the day star arise in our hearts. Knowing this first that no prophecy of scripture is of any private interpretation. For the prophecy came not in old time by the will of man: but holy men of God spake as they were*

> *moved by the Holy Ghost. (2 Peter 1: 19-21)*

Be humble in this area. Not every prophetic word has a direct correlation to the scripture. This is true for prophetic words that may deal with specific situations in your life. Be sure that the word given does not tell you to do anything against the Word.

Is it demonic, fleshly, or the Spirit of God? You must learn to recognize the source of the word. Is it in agreement with the will of God for your life?

> *Beloved, believe not every spirit, but try the spirits whether they are of God... (I John 4:1a)*

Please be wise in this area also. Sometimes, our own personal perceptions may

Exploring Questions & Answers for the Prophetic Office and Gift

hinder us from receiving from God. If we do not agree with a person's demeanor, we may say it was flesh.

Remember, God uses people. Their attributes and personality traits may surface as the Spirit moves through them. Let not your own biases block you from hearing from God.

Does it agree with previous prophetic revelation? Sometimes individuals may prophesy their own will for your life. They will say things that you have never heard concerning you or your life in God.

They may try to state prophetically that you are called to a ministry, or that you are supposed to take some sort of new direction in your life. When this happens, judge the word according to previous prophetic utterances from the Lord.

> *This command I entrust to you, Timothy, my son, in accordance with the prophecies previously made concerning you... (I Timothy 1:18a, NASB)*

However, just because someone tells you something that God may not have previously revealed to you does not mean it is not from the Lord. Our walks with the Lord are progressive and so is His revelation concerning our lives.

Sometimes God will reveal something "new" to us in order to guide us into the next phase of our relationship with Him. Be prayerful when new prophetic revelation is given to you. It may very well be the voice of the Lord.

The aforementioned guidelines are to help us in our efforts to receive from God. They are not to be used as excuses to reject the word of the Lord. Sometimes, there will be prophetic words given to which the guidelines may tell you to reject it, but you may discover that the word is from God. Be humble and prayerful while you are trying to judge the prophetic word.

Bibliography

Evans, Roderick L. Kingdom Practice, Power, and Principle Writers Club Press. Lincoln, NE, c2002

Lockman Foundation. Comparative Study Bible. Zondervan Publishing House. Grand Rapids, MI, c1984

Tucker, Ron & Hufton, Rick. God's Plan For Christian Service. Grace Church. St. Louis, MO, c1987

The Bible Library. The Bible Library CD Rom Disc. Ellis Enterprises Incorporated, (c) 1988 – 2000. 4205 McAuley Blvd., Suite 385,

Oklahoma City, OK 73120. All Rights Reserved.

Evans, Roderick L. (2014). The Prophetic Mantle: The Gift of Prophecy and Prophetic Operations in the Church Today. Camden, N.C. : Abundant Truth Publishing

Notes:

PROPHETIC CLARITY Exploring Questions & Answers for the Prophetic Office and Gift

Exploring Questions & Answers for the Prophetic Office and Gift

www.ingramcontent.com/pod-product-compliance
Lightning Source LLC
Chambersburg PA
CBHW050343010526
44119CB00049B/679